E N D U R A N C E

BOOKS BY DONALD FINKEL

Going Under *and* Endurance 1978

A Mote in Heaven's Eye 1975

Adequate Earth 1972

The Garbage Wars 1970

Answer Back 1968

A Joyful Noise 1966

Simeon 1964

The Clothing's New Emperor 1958
(IN POETS OF TODAY VI)

DONALD FINKEL

ENDURANCE

AN ANTARCTIC IDYLL

NEW YORK 1978 Atheneum

FOR CONNIE

Library of Congress Cataloging in Publication Data

Finkel, Donald.
Endurance: an Antarctic idyll.

I. Finkel, Donald. Going under. 1978. II. Title
PS3556.I48E5 1978 811'.5'4 78-55020
ISBN 0-689-10902-4

Published simultaneously in Canada by McClelland and Stewart Ltd.
Manufactured by American Book–Stratford Press,
Saddle Brook, New Jersey
Designed by Harry Ford
First Edition

CONTENTS

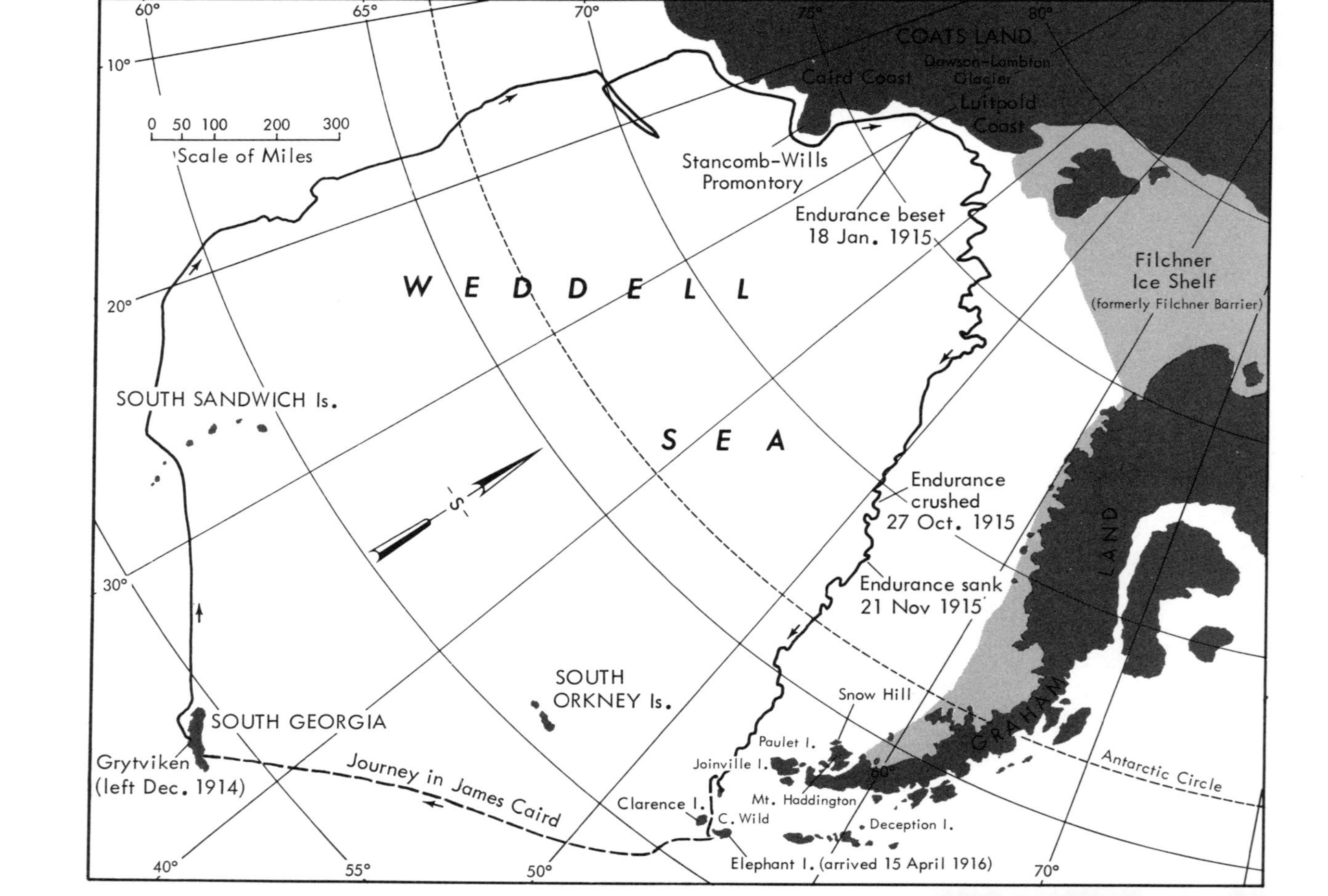
COATS LAND
Dawson-Lambton Glacier
Caird Coast
Luitpold Coast
Stancomb-Wills Promontory
Endurance beset 18 Jan. 1915
Filchner Ice Shelf
(formerly Filchner Barrier)
WEDDELL
SEA
SOUTH SANDWICH Is.
Scale of Miles
0 50 100 200 300
S
Endurance crushed 27 Oct. 1915
Endurance sank 21 Nov 1915
GRAHAM LAND
SOUTH ORKNEY Is.
SOUTH GEORGIA
Grytviken (left Dec. 1914)
Journey in James Caird
Snow Hill
Paulet I.
Joinville I.
Mt. Haddington
Clarence I.
C. Wild
Deception I.
Elephant I. (arrived 15 April 1916)
Antarctic Circle
60°
65°
70°
75°
80°
10°
20°
30°
40°
55°
50°
70°

A POINT OF DEPARTURE

On Dec. 5, 1914, Ernest Shackleton sailed on the *Endurance* from Grytviken, South Georgia, with the intention of landing a transcontinental expedition on the shore of the Weddell Sea. But, skirting the pack-ice in hopes of landing the crossing party as far south as possible, the *Endurance* found herself trapped between massive floes. For nine months she was swept irresistibly westward, then northward with the clockwise drift of the pack—until the pressure of millions of tons of thrusting pack proved too much, even for the *Endurance*. She was crushed to splinters.

Yet not until the twenty-eight survivors made ready to set up camp on the uncompromising surface of the pack did they truly begin to learn the meaning of endurance. For almost five months they suffered recurrent plagues of hunger, cold, blizzard, and boredom; then one week crouched in three small boats, battered by drift-ice, drenched in freezing spray—to land on Elephant Island, a large forsaken rock off the tip of the Antarctic Peninsula. There, twenty-two of the party were to remain four and one half months more, while Shackleton and five others (among them Harry McNeish, ship's carpenter, past fifty, the oldest man in the expedition, and hardly the soundest) pushed off for aid in the twenty-foot whaleboat *James Caird,* and recrossed in sixteen terrible days some 800 miles of the most treacherous sea in the world, to strike once more that inconsiderable speck, the island of South Georgia (from which they had departed on the *Endurance* a scarcely credible sixteen months before).

Even this was not to be the end of their ordeal, for they beached the *Caird* during a storm, no longer seaworthy, on the wrong side of the island. Between them and the whaling station lay miles of still-uncharted mountains and glaciers. Across that ragged landscape Shackleton, Worsley the skipper, and Crean the second officer trudged, clambered, stumbled and slid to safety. Though balked by the pack, another three months elapsed before he could manage it, Shackleton plucked every last man from the grip of the ice, leaving nothing behind but five of the stowaway Blackboro's toes.

For the details of this gloriously futile enterprise, there are available several excellent accounts—Shackleton's own *South*; Worsley's recently published narrative, *Shackleton's Boat Journey;* Margery and James Fisher's biography, *Shackleton and the Antarctic*; and Alfred Lansing's astonishing recreation, *Endurance.* To all of these, and to the manuscript diary of Harry McNeish the carpenter, I owe an incalculable debt.

There is little profit in contending with these volumes in respect to accuracy. It never occurred to me to try. I can only hope that, wherever in the course of this chronicle I have departed from the particulars, I have not compromised thereby the outlines of this remarkable journey.

ONE

An adventure is only an inconvenience rightly considered.
CHESTERTON

Reversal is the movement of Tao.
LAO-TSE

It's not good to do that kind of thing too often.
SHACKLETON

REMAINS

Beyond the shingle, under the bluff
turfed round with tussocks of dry grass
the upturned boat squats like a hermit's house

under the boat, the carpenter
straddling a narrow thwart
dabbles his ravaged toes in the glimmer-dark

gone to earth in his ark
a keel his roof, a sail his door
the old man tacks drowsily into Sunday morning

forward, Blackboro groans
in the grip of his dream-gale
the fisherman snores midships like distant surf

topside, a glacier roars, calving
from the icy shingle a bull sea-elephant replies
rats in the wainscot echo the question:

Do we build a house for ever?

THE JOURNEY

Mr. Freshfield: The great uncertain element in your progress is: what is the nature of the ground? You may come across a mountain range.
Sir E: There may be that, but I can always come back.
The President: I suppose you realize if you found such a range and explored it that it would really be much more interesting than a mere journey straight across?
Sir E: The journey across is the thing I want to do.

The whalers warned him from the beginning
ice had come far north that season
but he would have none of it

the morning we sailed, overcast
spitting snow
but we made good way

second morning, Holness yelled for Wild:
at the bottom of his locker, a pair of
black dress shoes stood, blinking under the 'skins

we hauled him up to the Boss
—What's your name boy?
—Blackboro

arms crossed, rocking
his great blue jaw raised like a fist:
—If we run out of food you'll be eaten first, hear?

a smile crept, hesitant, across Blackboro's lips
next day, south of Candlemas Island, we met
the outer ring of pack

the ice had come far north
in fact
farther than the whaler's whitest dreams

THE MAZE

1:

Pack-ice might be described as a gigantic and interminable jig-saw-puzzle devised by Nature. The parts of the puzzle in loose pack have floated slightly apart and become disarranged; at numerous places they have pressed together again

Round the cape of disappointment
south, through the wandering isles
past rocking cliffs
through fields of sea-ice
yellow with seal-piss and diatoms
the crew sang chanties
steaming down canyons of alabaster
a noisy cheerful lot of
trawler-hands and navvies
ferrying nine white knights
to the promised land

I have taken the liberty of calling the expedition "The Imperial Trans-Antarctic Expedition"

one month, nosing the pack
backing from false leads, ramming floes
inching southward, hugging the coast
but not too hard

on the thirty-second day
a blizzard, shrieking out of east-north-east
drove heavy snow off the Barrier slopes

three days in the lee of a stranded berg

2:

Grampa was a carpenter
slept on the bench when he was a boy

washed his face in cedar chips
trimmed his beard with a cross-cut saw

a stript abstract; an unfractioned integral; uncompromised as a new-born babe

Father ran a cabinet shop
knew a saw-horse from a handsaw
rubbed all day and half the night
to soothe the dowagers of Glasgow

(brushing with jewelled claws
the shimmering burl, the slow
convolutions of walnut)

but I scarpered off to sea
far from satinwood and pear
heart shakes, cankers and splay knots
where the waves roll clean and clear

(seven years on a coastal collier
cabin-boy and donkey-man
before I bobbed up like a chestnut scrap
by the carpenter's bench, where I belonged
where I rocked for thirty seasons more
but the days of wood were closing fast
in the gritty jaws of iron and smoke
when I heard the siren song of ice)

from the sentimental point of view, it is the last great Polar journey that can be made

3:

The gale abated:
three miles on, the lead gave out

far from the reek of furnished rooms
from white washstands, kneeling meekly
under cracked enamel ewers
far from dresser-scarves, antimacassars
and the fearful flanks of chambermaids

floes like none we'd seen
thick, soft, a sea of rotten brash
a cold green pudding closing round *Endurance*

4:

A fifty-year-old navigator off a tanker
laying out on the dresser of a 5-a-nite room
his billfold handkerchief comb key like a gypsy fortune
on the 200th birthday of New Jersey
may be said to endure

a seventy-three-year-old widow, catching
in her frail, asthmatic breast
her final breath
for the billionth time
may be said to endure

down the hall, the john sighs
the widow gasps, the scowling mariner
cracks the first of his still chill 6-pack
and settles on the edge of the bed
to endure, to ride out

one more night of dirty weather

5:

I was born beset
wind caught me in his fist, and squeezed

lapped in snowy bandages
clamped in the blinding vise of light
I lay on my back and crowed

how far have I drifted
trapped in the floes of circumstance?

DO WE

Low tide, light mist on the upper peaks
the carpenter crawls from his shell
and limps down the beach, past the basking seals

a cow rolls coyly onto her back
in the urine-dappled snow
to watch him pass

rounding the glacier-foot
a figurehead drifts into view
lacking one breast, a mermaid amazon

teak stanchions, richly carved
iron-bound timbers, mainyards, shattered masts
a child's boat, badly stove

he stoops to touch a broken oar, sea-silvered
running his thumb along the edge
of the stone-smooth blade

catches, in the tail of his eye
a flash of sunlight hurled from the brow of the cliff
into the cloudless morning

straightens, shouldering his booty
and hobbles up the snow-slope, whistling:
—*Do we do we do we do we*

TWO

TRADING TRADES

Wednesday Mar 24th Lat 76-26S temp Minus 9. 2 dogs shot today we had the dredge down & got some Antipodes & stone

After a week, we damped the fires
let the boilers cool
at the end of five, gave up ship's hours
and slept the night through

high on the mast, one watchman
scoured the horizon
landscape of magnificent wreckage
hemming us in

in the south, the night sun
hovered over the Barrier
casting a queer light on the icebergs
a ghost armada, gliding with us
imperceptibly westward

atop the cabin, blinking her violet eyes
a black-and-white cat lay
watching the watchman

The meteorologist had got his recording station, containing anemometer, barograph, and thermograph, rigged over the stern. The geologist was making the best of what was to him an unhappy situation, but it was not altogether without material. The pebbles found in the penguins were often of considerable interest

while the firemen carted ice
while the fisherman trawled for stones
while Blackboro, turned cabin-boy
played hide-and-seek with a seal
round a stranded berg

while, weather permitting
the skipper and Wild took the dogs for a run

deep between-decks
Jonah in a grounded whale
I labored
making over, making do
transforming voyage to asylum
contriving a winter palace
of packing crates and two-by-fours

Teeth he accounted bits of ivory; heads he deemed but top-blocks; men themselves he lightly held for capstans.

spoke to no one but the cat
my motto, Mind the corners
sides will mind themselves

CRUMBS

Tuesday June 22nd Midwinter Day A lovely morning Lat 74-21 S Temp Minus 14 we had sausages & onions fried for Breakfast & it was a treat after being so long on seal & penguin meat

Hunched over the bench, caressing
a ten-inch scrap of English oak
with the sole of his plane
raising pale gold spirals the length of the stroke
gracing the air with a tang of bitter tea
I shaped a cribbage board
for the navigator

the grain streamed down the board like fleeting years
swirling all but unimpeded round
a single dark, contracted spot
still brooding, where the woodsman's ax
sheared cleanly the offending limb

again, again
riding the current down
the jack-plane struck the sullen knot
and shot bravely through

dinner at 6 Roast Pork stewed apples & preserved peas with plum pudding & we had a concert which started at 8 & finished at 12 PM with fried onions & bread then we drank the health of our Loved Ones at Home

topside, six hours of twilight
pink glow in the north at noon
no land in sight

fresh southerly breeze
the nostrils crackled and sang
fair light from the friendly moon

the south shook out
her glimmering apron
scattering crumbs of grace

FOOTPRINTS

Four sets of footprints going up, one coming back
clear as the morning they appeared
close at the heels of the silent men

three pairs marked by screws
drawn from the boat
eight in each boot, he knows without counting

(drove them into their wretched soles himself
with the broken blade of his pocket-knife
and hobbled beside them halfway up the slope)

the old man comes to a trampled place
the footprints merge and
sort themselves out

he watches the marked three climbing on
over the coruscating ridges
into the mountains of indifference

PRESSURE

1:
started to build a wheelhouse on the poop it will be a good thing for the steersman and it is also using up the timber we have left

Wrestling a length of pine up the companionway
I met Himself, coming down:
the gentleman pressed against the rail
noblesse oblige, to let me pass

genial, easy, undismayed
insufferably cheerful
—What was he good for?
I asked the board

that even-handed, open-hearted
rosy-breasted schoolboy
what can you make of a smile?
what can you build with a grin?

grappling the seven-foot board like a lubberly angel
I staggered up through the starlit hatch
the light wind licked my eyes
at each corner a tear glinted like amethyst

heavy with cold, the wind streamed down
a thousand glittering miles to the Barrier
picking up speed, and
slammed into the sea-ice like a sledge

waves of impact shuddered toward *Endurance*

And it grew wondrous cold

2:

Time was, the glacier
licked him into shape
with her cruel tongue

her whelp, the irritable ape
his teeth were sharpened
on the stones of fear

asleep in the mountain's palm
she grinds her teeth
she is dreaming of him

a species of sullen, combative, self-conscious, fiercely adaptable predators

time will be again
she will return, scourge of the hills
scouring the valleys clean

3:
All through the winter the drifting pack changes—grows by freezing, thickens by rafting, and corrugates by pressure. If, finally in its drift it impinges on a coast, such as the western shore of the Weddell Sea, a terrific pressure is set up

A slaughtered seal, left on the ice
will sink, in time
into the body of the floe

matchless crystals form, reform
relinquishing their intransigent boundaries
the vast shield bends under its own immensity

grinding the continent's belly:
chill black silver trickles
down her crevices

under sufficient pressure
everything flows

4:

While earth revolved in the socket of the dark
while heaven bent its starry knee
while the sea slid backward, and the pack
partaking of her vast reluctance
ground ponderously clockwise, carrying
Endurance northward, to her limit

deep in my splintery grotto
a sour Hephaestus, steaming like a peddler's nag
I pressed my chisel to the whirling stone
beating time with my foot on the rocking treadle

stars flew from my hand
winked out on the wool of my night-blue sleeve

5:

At the cost of his toes, a man endures
the kit-fox creeps off, leaving
her bloody paw in the teeth of the trap

the lichen and the stone endure
the Emperor sheers off, leaving his dam
in the teeth of the seal

at the cost of the flesh, the flesh endures
swimmer in the greasy cross-chop
rabbit in the snare

HUNTING

the mass of biological material on the surface of the Earth is only a few times 10^{17} gm. according to the best recent estimates; less than 0.01 per cent of the mass of the Earth. Thus, for all our feelings of self-importance, we are only a kind of biological rust, clinging to the surface of our small planet

He strays from the trodden path
beating to starboard
up the slow rise to the top of the bluff

low in the east, the indifferent sun
rising out of hidden Husvik
bedazzles the bay

below, by the boat-house, house-boat
stooping double like a crone in a kitchen garden
the fisherman yanks the tough dry stalks of tussock-grass

nearby, sprawling against the bow
the boy exposes to the bitter light
his mouldering toes

and everywhere, swarming the stones
the voluptuous seals!
more meat than three hopeless men can eat in a year

swimming in plentitude, a sudden
dizziness assails him:
reeling back from the edge, he sets off again

THREE

THE SHIP

1:
September 30 was a bad day. It began well, for we got two penguins and five seals during the morning. Three other seals were seen. But at 3 p.m. cracks that had opened during the night alongside the ship commenced to work in a lateral direction. The ship sustained terrific pressure on the port side forward, the heaviest shocks being under the fore-rigging. It was the worst squeeze we had experienced. The decks shuddered and jumped, beams arched, and stanchions buckled and shook.

Passing my cranny, young Blackboro
clutched the doorjamb and
set down his bucket of seal livers

I looked up from my vise at the deck-beam
bending like a piece of cane
and cursed the day I signed my name

near me, on the bench
the cat hunched
paws tucked under, in a trance of fear

2:
Overhead the sun shone serenely; occasional fleecy clouds drifted before the southerly breeze, and the light glinted and sparkled on the million facets of the new pressure-ridges. The day passed slowly. At 7 p.m. very heavy pressure developed, with twisting strains that racked the ship fore and aft.

At ten, a band of Emperors called

all month, we'd seen them
never so many
in pairs, threes, or alone

urging themselves with little cries
hobbling into the heart of cold

now, gathered in the half-light
nine or ten of them
fixing us with their obsidian eyes
uttered a chorus of weird, disconsolate cries:
the Emperors were singing

—Hear that? the fisherman muttered
to no one in particular
we'll none of us
get back to our homes again

3:

This morning, our last on the ship, the weather was clear, with a gentle south-south-easterly to south-south-westerly breeze. From the crow's nest there was no sign of land of any sort. The pressure was increasing steadily, and the passing hours brought no relief or respite for the ship. The attack of the ice reached its climax at 4 p.m. The ship was hove stern up by the pressure, and the driving floe, moving laterally across the stern, split the rudder and tore out the rudder-post

To the east, an enormous train with squeaky axles
shunted toward some terrible siding

moaning, whining, sirens of ice
clutched at us

in the distance, a cock crowed
a muffled roll of drums

the puzzle pieces were coming together of themselves

The pumps work faster and faster and someone is actually singing a chanty to their beat. The dogs are rapidly passed down a canvas chute and secured on the floe, followed by cases of concentrated sledging rations, sledges and equipment. The ship is doomed.

at five, the word came down:
—Abandon ship

I turned from my post at the coffer-dam
and made my way along the canted passage

at the door of my lair, I paused and leaned inside
peering at the wreck of my occupation

In ultimate analysis, the practical truth rests upon the certainty that all the laws of the inanimate universe are hostile to organic life.

the bench, sprung free
wobbled toward me on jointless legs

brashy water swirled round its feet
bobbing with scraps of hardwood, maple pegs

thrusting through the side
a ragged tongue of ice gleamed hungrily

beside it, arching on the topmost shelf
tail flared, indignant and erect

the cat glared back

4:

Three-masted, a stately barkentine
slim as a schooner aft
full-rigged before
Endurance came on like a queen

seven feet of solid oak
sheathed in greenheart, hard as iron
from stem to stern

her ice-sheathed rigging
twanged like harpstrings
her timbers snapped to the floor-plates'
screech and clang

what was the song *Endurance* sang?

5:
We had a long arm with an electric cluster, over where the dogs were. Something set that off, and you could hear the ship being crushed, and suddenly a light went on for a moment and then went out. It seemed the end of everything.

A silent fare-thee-well
to my bench and my vise
to my faithful rasps
my files and try-squares
my awls, my augers
tranquil spirit levels
imperturbable planes

into your hand are they delivered

then I gentled the cat
to my shoulder
and went topside

THE ANGEL

1:
Living in unobstructed space, they have little occasion for tight maneuvers or sudden stops. When they land on their nesting grounds, which they can only do in flat open areas, they have difficulty reducing their speed

In a patch of tussock-grass, three shallow nests
in each, a soot-grey fledgling albatross
fat as a full-grown hen

planting his oar, he lifts the first:
the shrivelled webs
dangle obscenely from his fingers

his heart is drenched in a primordial chill
he catches his breath, then
clamps the neck in his grime-black fist and

wrenches clockwise
tightening
tightening

2:
If there had been foxes in Polynesia, and on the islands farther south, or primitive men, such large birds would hardly have found sites safe for breeding

Cramming the corpse in his greasy coat
he does for the second
bending for the last, he hears

the scream, descending
reaches for the oar instead
upright in the snow, handle toward his hand

the angel hurtles to meet him
black primaries rattling
tail spread fanwise, braking wildly

so that the wanderers sometimes tip up on their noses and tumble over before coming to a stop.

THE KNOT

1:

A man must shape himself to a new mark directly the old one goes to ground.

Tossing three sovereigns on the moonlit snow
our leader drew his pocket watch
and pitched that too
then took up his bible and
tore out the page from *Job*:

Out of whose womb came the ice?
And the hoary frost of Heaven, who hath engendered it?
The waters are hid as with a stone,
And the face of the deep is frozen.

dropped the book at his feet
that lantern-jawed Episcopalian Argonaut
and strode away, not looking back
while each of us in turn
pitched onto the growing mound chronometers
axes chisels telescopes letters all
but the clothes on our backs
two pair of boots and a sleeping bag
and followed on his heels
to the restless dogs, panting by the sledges

2:

The bloody dogs
yelping in the traces
lunging up hedgerows of pressure
yanking the clumsy sledge

or curled under drifts
tail over muzzle, sleeping

dreamless as teeth
in the jaw of the storm

granted, their cruelty and greed
what I could not forgive
was their clownish, incorrigible
malevolence

As a matter of fact the cat could have come along with us in splendid style had it not been that the dogs, now that she lacked the protection of the ship, would have eaten her.

behind the berg, four shots:
Sallie's youngest pups
too small to pull

then one shot more

It has a distinctly pathetic side, but it is good to know clearly that they have not the intelligence to anticipate their fate

wilder than the dogs
and more civil
the cat had kept her distance
padding down the farthest
reaches of *Endurance*
where could she stalk in peace?
where could she crawl in fear
on that ill-begotten ice?

3:

Welding the long-boat to the motor sledge
pounding on a starboard brace
I heard Himself behind me
curse and call:

—Here Chips come here and
hold this bloody dog

into your hand are they delivered

well into my fiftieth year
driven like a coffin nail
I struck the knot

—Hold him yourself, I said

4:
All members of the crew without exception to have interchangeable duties and to perform any duty on board in the boats, or on the shore

What shore?

by the last of the ship
in whose name we swore
caught fast in that unearthly plain
like a hillock of fruitless trees

What is the nature of the ground?

it was not death I feared
but dying piecemeal
tools, trade, falling away
like blackened fingers

my eyeteeth moaned in my skull
my white breath shivered
on the wind's blue cheek
and fell in glittering shards

on that groundless ground
that corpse of water
terra infirma, kingdom of zero
rocking between cold and cold

THE BATTLE

Flailing the wounded oar like a cricket bat
he catches her offside elbow, sends her
spinning over the lip

long moments later, creaking her ponderous wings
the angel reappears
wheeling into the teeth of the wind, still screaming

he crams the last of the nestlings into his parka
shoulders his weapon and sounds retreat:
—*Do we do we!*

head craning
one arm outstretched for balance
a ragged penguin, shambling over the trackless crust

F O U R

PATIENCE

1:

The second Christmas sought me out
crouched in the small hours
sent three Emperors calling at our tent-flap

I crept from my pallet, fumbling for the club:
they gathered to greet me, bearing on their backs
rich oil and thrice-blessed flesh

the wind was blowing out of the south
too light to stir the pack
a seal lay watching by his blowhole
having no knees, he could not kneel
psalms rose on plumes of breath
as I crept child-wise over the ignorant snow

what can you nail to a canvas wall?

at six we loaded our gifts on the sledges and fled
into the jaws of the wilderness
behind us the ghost of *Endurance* moaned
a pale cat's-cradle of frozen cordage

who can fashion the hinges of ice?

2:

Friday Dec 31st Hogmany & a bitter one too being adrift on the ice instead of enjoying the pleasures of life like wise people but as the saying is there must be some fools in this world.

Worsley called it Mark Time Camp
Himself preferred to call it Patience
and Patience it was
a strong old floe, seven miles
from the leavings of *Endurance*

Hurley & Boss play religiously a set of six games of poker patience every afternoon. I think each rather regards it as a duty but it certainly passes away an hour.

(it beat man-hauling:
leaning in harness
up to the knees in
soft wet snow
tugging the boat-sledge
that humped hermaphrodite
on stale thin bannock and weak cocoa
twenty yards, and a breather
seven miles in seven days)

Day passes day with very little or nothing to relieve the monotony. We take constitutionals round and round the floe but no one can go further as we are to all intents and purposes on an island. There is practically nothing fresh to read and nothing to talk about, all topics being absolutely exhausted.

sitting on our heels
grumbling in the tents
a tribe without women or children
licking our knives
lighting our pipes with pages
from the *Britannica*

Hussey is busy at present with his 6 tunes which is heart-breaking

slumped in torpor
stirring the canvas
with senseless breath
a straggle of nomads
camped on a floating
desert that nothing
with roots could survive

3:

65° 16½′ S, 52° 4′ W. No news.
S.E. wind, fine weather.
Patience,
Patience,
Patience.

4:

Still weather
sun circled his sky-blue cage
spiralling down and down

surrounded by leads too wide for the sledges
too tight for the boats
we drifted northward, grudgingly
past the Circle

5:

A skua gull appeared. He settled down on our refuse pit—entrails of seals, etc.—and gorged himself to his hearts content—lucky gull.

At breakfast, Greenstreet tipped his milk
whirled on Clark, roaring
fell silent, as suddenly
staring into the empty mug

wordless, Clark leaned over
poured into it some of his own
then Macklin, then the rest

under sufficient pressure

each in turn
swept into the act
rapt in the ice-clear silence

everything flows

6:
There has been a large swell since yesterday. But it is doing us no harm now our floe is broken up so small. It rises and falls with

That day I wrote no further:
floe cracked under the *Caird*
we tumbled out and
beached her anew

breakfast of dog-pemmican
watching lanes of open water steadily widening
suddenly Boss cried
—Strike the tents!

even as we ran, the floe
cracked the other way
ate lunch standing up
seal soup and powdered milk

at one, he nodded:
—Launch the boats
I ran to the *Caird*
snatched up the painter and began to pull

COMING HOME

It is the boy who hails him
home from the hill, his cry
flutters on the breeze like a flag of breath

kneeling by the peevish fire, feeding it
scraps of driftwood, morsels of dry grass
the fisherman does not lift his head to see

the carpenter set down his oar
unsheathe his breast, and let his trophies fall
then limp to the long-house, slump beside the boy

the sun blinks, cheerless
over their shoulders
at the desolate bay:
frigates of glittering crystal, dreadnoughts of glass

ALBATROSS GRAVY

The manner of their flight proclaims the rule of law.

Seven years, riding the thermals
skimming the froth on the jaws of water

seven years between land and land
star of passage, angel of dirty weather

hunched on the mountain's shoulder, ponderous grace
dragging your glorious vans in the guano

brooding on the future's cool, unlovely
bland, inconsequential face

blessed are your children, awash in the hoosh-pot
swimming in heavenly gravy

FIVE

THE CROSSING

1:

Working down widening leads, toward the open sea
overladen (twelve in the *Caird*
eight in the *Docker,* seven in the *Wills*)
the boats rode low in the hungry cross-chop
spray glazing the oars

As I look back I cannot help wondering how we should have felt had we known the ordeals that awaited us, the dangers and disappointments we were destined to experience. At that time, when we had been living in a world of ice for so long, we could not imagine that there were situations still worse than those we had already faced.

free of the pack
which blunts the corners of water
it was worse by far
the seas came everywhichway
bristling with angry brash

we crouched in the *Caird,* watching
Wild in the bow
poling off growlers with a broken spar

2:

Nights camped on rocking floes
nights grappled to bergs
by the treacherous ice-foot
killers blowing

nights sitting up in the boats
too cold to sleep, too stiff to lie down
lips cracked and swollen
chewing seal meat for the salty blood

fifth day, dawn dragged her
belly across the horizon

shook the reef from our sails
running before the wind
through loose pack

thousands of little dead fish lay
glazed and gleaming
on the green, rubbery
skin of the sea

dove-grey skuas
stooped to take them up

3:

And one last night in the boats
a heavy sea running
plunging through spindrift
heeling, close to the wind

an hour before midnight, the moon
broke through a cloud-rift:
I can still see him
poised in the stern

in his left hand
the ice-sheathed line
that ran to the *Wills*
wallowing behind us like a stricken whale

right hand firm on the tiller
keeping us into the wind
though the moon danced on his shoulder
like a drunken boat

at six, Wild went to spell him
and dragged him forward

chafing his loins, to loose them
from their rigor

I slipped my hand under his brittle clothes
and felt in his breast
his blind heart stumbling
doggedly on

O thou of little faith, wherefore didst thou doubt

4:
And the wind ceased, and there was a great calm.

Some kneeling some reeling some
staggering with laughter
some playing with little
sea-smooth stones

now and again one
fell to his knees then
grave and deliberate
rose once more to

will you won't you
join the dance
prancing on the shingle
like a drunken faun

Boss looked on, smiling
at his right hand
the tranquil seals
lolled on the shore

by his left, through a cleft
through the glacier's
dreaming fingers trickled
a rivulet of living water

my cup runneth over

THE KNIFE

His universe of instruments is closed and the rules of his game are always to make do with 'whatever is at hand'

Kneeling at Blackboro's naked stone-grey foot
the fisherman takes it in his lap:
five black stumps on a hillock of ashes

bereft of its nail
the great toe blooms
blue-black, moist as a camelia

with glacier-tears, boiled in a billy-can
the fisherman laves the cadaverous limb
gingerly, lest he offend a single part

the old fabricator wipes his mouth on a sleeve
grunts to his feet and grumbles down
to rinse his pocket-knife in the healing wave

THE BOAT

1:

The 20-ft. boat had never looked big; she appeared to have shrunk in some mysterious way when I viewed her in the light of our new undertaking. She was an ordinary ship's whaler, fairly strong, but showing signs of the strains she had endured since the crushing of the Endurance. *Where she was holed in leaving the pack was, fortunately, above the water line and easily patched. Standing beside her, we glanced at the fringe of the storm-swept, tumultuous sea that formed our path. Clearly, our voyage would be a big adventure. I called the carpenter and asked him if he could do anything*

With hickory runners from the dismantled sledge
with box-lids and stiff canvas
thawed, inch by inch
on the blubber fire
with halfpenny nails
prized from the packing cases
screws from *Endurance*
I patched her together
caulked her with lamp-wick
raised her and rigged her
to weather the crossing

I started to dismantle the Docker *to deck in the* Caird *which is going to South Georgia for relief as I dont think there will be many survivors if they have to put in a winter here.*

—Let me go, I said
he was standing behind me
I could feel his eyes
parting my shoulderblades

I looked up from my work:

—Let me go
gazing into those blue holes, I said
—Sir

and he did

2:

Second night out, the small nails
crept from their holes
pools of ice-black water
gathered on the sagging canvas
trickling down where I lay
shivering on the ballast in my sodden bag
a sack of bones atop a sack of stones
and heard, mid the tumult
the little nails complaining:

Do we build a house for ever?

3:

Fourth day, wind so fierce
we hove to, double-reefed
fifth day worse

spray froze as it struck the bow
sheath on sheath of gleaming mail
we clambered over her, chipping and scraping

sixth day, lost sea-anchor:
nothing for it but
beat ice from the sail and raise it
gear protesting, fingers hideous with blisters
thighs scraped raw in our sodden clothes

the sea rubbed salt in our wounds

4:

Wind eased in the night

seventh morning, the prodigal sun returned
all hands turned out to pipe him back
basking like seals
round whom the grinning dolphins leapt

pied cape pigeons, clapping their lath-wings, wheeled
or rocked beside us, comfortable as ducks
one rose on unlikely legs, beam to the wind
skittering over the skin of the sea

from swollen mouths
gurgling past cracked lips
black laughter spilled

5:

Three days hard wind, good way
eleventh day, a stiff southwesterly
sky lowering, snow squalls, a cross-sea going

midnight at the tiller, Boss made out
a line of white sky in the south:
—It's clearing! he called

a moment later I realized what I had seen was not a rift in the clouds but the white crest of an enormous wave. During twenty-six years' experience of the ocean in all its moods I had not encountered a wave so gigantic. It was a mighty upheaval of the ocean, a thing quite apart

solid, like the ice
a white intelligence
vast, dim as the vaults of leviathan

lifted and flung us
swallowed the boat and
spat it out

I don't think that any of us were conscious of actual fear of death. I know that I did have, however, a very disagreeable, cold sort of feeling, quite different from the physical chill that I suffered. It was a sort of mental coldness.

flailing the hoosh-pot
feeding water to water
I glared at the gunwhale

ice blinked back from the oarlock in the roaring dark

6:
The morning of May 8 broke thick and stormy, with squalls from the north-west. We searched the waters ahead of us for a sign of land, and though we could see nothing more than had met our eyes for many days, we were cheered by a sense that the goal was near at hand. About ten o'clock that morning we passed a little bit of kelp

Watched at noon the black cliffs
rise from their graves
attended by petrels
bearded with tussock-grass
grey-green in the gathering dusk
up to their knees in the barbarous surf

all day, all night
stood away on a starboard tack
goaded by salt
mouths so dry we could not eat
drinking water brackish, the cask being stove
thick with reindeer hair from the sleeping bags

I can see him now, in the grey light
holding under his sweater, to his naked breast
Blackboro's leprous foot
can hear the fisherman curse the frozen shrouds
and Crean, faithful Crean
singing at the tiller

He always sang while he was steering, and nobody ever discovered what the song was. It was devoid of tune and as monotonous as the chanting of a Buddhist monk at his prayers; yet somehow it was cheerful.

7:

We went to sea in a sieve, we did
for sixteen days six simpletons
six ninnies jiggling in a coffin
six splinters in the thumb of chaos
bobbed and wallowed, dipped and dithered
floundered foundered shivered singing:

Twankedillo, Twankedillo,
And a roaring pair of bagpipes
Made from the green willow.

when we beached her at last
we stripped her topsides for a fire
bathing our battered hands in the greasy smoke

8:
It would seem that mythological worlds have been built up, only to be shattered again, and that new worlds were built from the fragments

With a crippled boy
a snoring fisherman

with an ark turned turtle
resurrected nails
whatever comes to hand
I patch my saga

with a rudder for ripsaw
the mast my only tree
I follow the grain
wherever it flows
trimming the stern
to piece out the bow

I'm down to my bones Grandfather

SLEEP

sleep on now, and take your rest: it is enough

Eyes half closed
he strokes his pocket-knife
on a sea-smooth stone
the tide of sleep laps round his knees

caress of static
wind through invisible leaves
the rasp of silk on silk
kiss kiss of inconceivable thighs

it is enough
this shore, this garden of stones
these companions, these
rags on the hem of bedlam

this shoal of flesh
the scent on your lips
sweet flesh
it will suffice

SIX